HEAL
THYSELF

WHITE EAGLE

THE WHITE EAGLE PUBLISHING TRUST
LISS · HAMPSHIRE · ENGLAND

MCMLXXIX

First Edition: November 1962
Reprinted: April 1969
Reprinted: May 1973
Reprinted: October 1976
Reprinted: April 1978
Reprinted: November 1979

ISBN 0 85487 015 6

Printed in Great Britain by
Fletcher & Son Ltd, Norwich

CONTENTS

Foreword

This book would point the way to the source of all healing, a way that has been tested and proven by time. For nearly half a century White Eagle, through Mrs. Grace Cooke, has been healing the sick in mind and body, as well as teaching others how to heal, and over the years we have witnessed countless quiet miracles, not only of bodily healing but of changed lives. Because of this we know that his way, when followed faithfully, leads to a new life.

It may help you to enter into the spirit of the words and especially into the spirit of the communion with which the book ends, if you will picture the surroundings in which these words were spoken.

Visualise the quiet chapel with its plain white walls and simple furnishings; the raised altar, pure white against a background of blue velvet; the lighted candles, the flowers, and a copy of the St. John's Cross on Iona, carved in limed oak. See the symbol of the white eagle suspended above the altar, and the light shining down upon its outstretched wings to flood the altar.

We become conscious of a presence, an almost indescribable power, as White Eagle slowly rises to give his message. As we listen, anxiety, tribulation, and ills of the flesh lose their hold; we are quickened in spirit and for a brief hour live in a more perfect world; we are enfolded in a great compassionate love—the love which heals.

I

The Life-Giving Spirit

We come from the world of spirit to bring a message of love and hope. You all suffer in various ways; some from pain and inconveniences of the flesh, some from torment of the mind; others are disturbed in soul, anxious, fearful, perhaps at times angry. We come to comfort and inspire you, and to tell you that these trials under which you suffer are but means used, lessons given to you, to prepare you for the land of beauty and opportunity, the land of heavenly bliss.

We are not unaware of the disappointments and fears that possess you, the hardships you endure. We in spirit know you have tests. We know the physical body is not always as fit and perfect as it could be; we know the material conditions of your life can be tiresome. Do not think that we have no feeling for earthly things. We are so attuned to you that we absorb your feelings, we understand the problems and difficulties; but we come to tell you that there is a life within you which can prevail over the flesh, and to show you how, by your own effort, you can realise it.

2

All human life is governed by divine law, and although you may endure pain while in your physical body, we hope that you will do so with courage and that you will accept the problems that face you, not exactly as a challenge, but as an opportunity from which you can learn wisdom and attain mastery. These experiences constitute a discipline, sent to you not by God, as some people think, but by the law of *cause* and *effect*; for you yourselves at some time and place have sown the seed. You have made yourself what you are; and it is no use blaming God or anyone else.

Yet God has put in your hands the remedy for all your ills. The Lord Christ brought this to humanity when he said, 'Love one another.' To love is to fulfil the law.

Love *is* the law; it is life; and when you put the law into operation everything works together for good in your life. When you love, you are in direct contact with the Christ spirit, and there is no darkness in you.

3

We would help you to rise and attain freedom from the bondage of earth while you still have the use of a physical body.

But do not make any mistake: life on earth is a valuable, an indispensable experience; and you have to learn to preserve your physical body in health by living in harmony with natural and divine law. When these laws are broken through some weakness in himself, man suffers. The body is of God and needs to be treated with respect and consideration, to be loved. To love another helps him to rise to perfection. Love your body then. Do not overwork, overstrain, overfeed or over-indulge it, for Christ Himself depends on it as a vehicle that He can use in the service of all creation. You have a solemn duty to care for it, to treat it gently and wisely, to purify it, because it is meant to be a temple of the living Christ. It is not to be regarded as something from which to escape. The forces of light and darkness are at work in it, and by your own will, which operates from the heart of love, you can bring the Christ Light into manifestation in every atom.

You are spirit. The real you, the consciousness, is spirit. As you strengthen this realisation through meditation and worship of your Creator your spirit will begin to dominate the physical atoms, until your body becomes irradiated with life, and every particle obeys the direction of spirit, the real you.

4

While you live only in consciousness of the physical life around you, it is as if you were in a closed box, looking out through a dark window. Because of this, you grow weary and need help and reassurance; you long to rise beyond the limitations of earth, to get a clearer vision of the world of the spirit, which is not far from you, and which is indeed your true home, the home from which you came to dwell in the flesh.

We are permitted to come to you from the world of spirit to bring you that power which will lift you up and give peace of mind, strength of body.

But it is not enough that we bring you the power; you on your part must strive to realise your true life. You believe in an invisible life, an invisible power which will heal you of aches and pains, inharmonies, confusion; but this power needs to have a point of entry. You have to prepare your body, your mind, your soul for the inflow of this divine healing. There are many who seek healing without recognising this funda-mental truth that they are spirit; that they have as much to do with their own healing as any healer who tries to help them. It is not in accord with divine law for the body to be healed completely without the soul's co-operation. Before the body can be wholly restored you must play your part; the soul must learn the lesson sickness was designed to teach. Pray therefore that you may understand the cause and purpose of your sickness or unhappiness; and remember that whatever your karma it is good, it is an opportunity given you by divine law to grow in spirit.

mind?

Whatever your ill, its cause is the same, and the Power that heals is the same. But God moves in mysterious ways to perform miracles and uses many ways to heal, to repair the life, to open the vision, to develop the character and bring man's soul at last to the realisation of His glory.

5

Try to realise that you are not your physical body any more than you are the clothes you wear. Your body can be likened to your dress; and when your time for the great transition comes you will lay it aside as you lay aside your outworn clothes. But your true, your invisible self lies deep within you, covered up not only by the coat of skin but by other bodies such as the etheric, the emotional, the mental bodies. Think of peeling off these as you might peel off your garments, one by one;

and there, deep in the heart-centre, beneath these many layers, is the light, son of the Father-Mother God, most pure and holy. He is only a babe as yet and needs to grow to maturity, to be man-made-perfect, the Christ-Man.

When you turn to this inmost centre, this pure spirit, which is all love, you open the way for the inflow of the Christ healing. This works in several ways. You may have a pain which could be removed by the 'white magic' instantly; but that may not be what your soul needs. Bodily sickness is the result of inharmony in the soul: thus, to restore bodily health we must work through the soul, or there will only be a patching-up, a temporary relief. Spiritual healing works not only on your body but on your soul and your very life; there is a slow permeation of body and soul by the Christ spirit, the pure healing power. It will guide you always to choose the good, the beautiful and the true; to be tolerant and forgiving, patient and trustful. All these attributes will gradually develop in the soul that trusts faithfully in God's healing power.

6

The spirit can change the vibration of the physical body, of matter, and the heart of man is the receptacle for the inflow of spirit, which in simple terms is love. Let no man make the mistake of thinking that he is only human and cannot therefore be expected to respond to the purity of divine love. Man is divine as well as human. Jesus was man but he was also irradiated by Christ the Son.

Christ when manifesting through Jesus said, 'I am the resurrection and the life.' If man will seek the presence of Christ, who is the life-spirit of this world, he will receive perfect healing. Christ is the life, the life-force, the life-giving spirit, which flows through man's mind and soul into his etheric body, which is sometimes called a body of light, and is the transmitter of life-force to the physical body. Do not allow the earth mind to darken this body, for it is your soul-clothing. As you learn to love truly, your etheric body becomes a body of light and shines radiantly through the physical garment, giving it life and health, and through it—through you—life and sustenance to every soul you encounter, and you are thereby blessed.

Seek often this contact with the divine life. Through prayer and meditation seek fuller knowledge of the inner worlds, the beautiful joyous life of the spirit. Draw close to the Golden Light, the Master of Love, and reverently accept the sustenance He offers.

Realise the Spirit within You

We remind you again and again that God does not inflict suffering but uses the suffering man creates for himself to bring good into the individual life. Through changing conditions in the earth and in the elements above the earth the seed of life germinates, takes root, and in time grows into the perfect flower.

The lily that raises its head from the still water and opens to the warmth and light of the sun has its roots deep in the mud at the bottom of the pond. Human life is the same. But if you would become whole it is first necessary to forget your roots and the mud in which they are nourished, to think only of the light to which you are reaching, the beauty and strength of God.

When you are sick and weary, seek the presence of the Christ, the Golden One; draw His love, His strength, His beauty, into your soul.

To each of you He gives assurance that your life is working to a plan. The most important thing is for you to keep your sure contact with Him. If you do this nothing can go wrong; you will have no need to worry whether to do this, that or the other; your decisions will be made for you. But you must awaken to the spirit, you must be quickened in spirit, so that you may respond instantly to the gentle guidance of the almighty Presence in your heart.

The Holy Grail is the ever-burning flame that shines in your heart.

Keep this light burning steadily in your heart. We say this to you so often because we know it is the only thing that can help you in your human life. There is much to distract your mind and disturb your emotions; but always remind yourself that within you is this Light, this Presence, which has all power over your thoughts and feelings, your body and your material conditions.

2

When you can learn to withdraw at will from the outer confusion and conflict of human life into the peace of your age-long spirit, you will become strong to overcome physical disorders. You all have problems and anxieties, but you do not yet understand that you create them yourselves, and have the power within you to overcome them.

Some of you pray earnestly for your problems to be removed. You long for the coming of the light and for spiritual ecstasy; but, little ones, can you not see that it is only by undergoing the discipline of these outer things that your eyes are opened and your sensitivity to the heavenly truth increased? You cannot taste and see until you have passed through this process of discipline. Therefore thank God for all the irritations and heartaches, which come to discipline your soul until it can absorb and comprehend the beauty of the heavenly life.

As you go about in the world, do not forget those silent moments when, in the quiet of your inmost sanctuary, you have felt a spiritual power, the touch of angels' wings. In the stress of the world keep the sweetness of the Christ spirit ever with you. Let the world, with all its conflicts, its selfishness and ignorance, go by, and keep in your heart the sweetness of the heavenly life. We all need patience one with another; therefore be patient with those around you, be good in thought towards your fellows. This is the way to develop awareness of the invisible worlds and the heavenly states of life.

You cannot do more than live as Christ taught you to live, tranquilly and in his spirit. Do not try to do more than is humanly possible. Train yourselves to do one thing at a time, quietly, calmly. What you cannot accomplish is in God's hands, and God will take care of it. All He expects of His children is that they do their best in the most harmonious and loving way.

Do your best quietly and you will be working in accordance with that divine law which will 'make crooked places straight,' and restore harmony and health.

3

If you would be well and happy, give first attention to God, to the spirit. The body pulls very hard. Material things loom very big. Troubles crowd in and threaten to overwhelm you, but all these things are shadows. The time will come when you will recognise this truth even if you cannot accept it now. We tell you from the spirit that these things of earth are illusory, and the only thing which is real, which will live beyond physical death, is the spirit of God in you; for you are spirit and you are a child of God. God's love for you is beyond all human comprehension; it is all-enfolding and will never fail you so long as you look to it. It will sustain you, my children, through every ordeal you are called on to face. We cannot remind you too often that the trials of the flesh and material life which you endure are sent that you may gain wisdom from the experience. God is the great Architect of the universe, and He does not play havoc with His material. He builds according to the true law. He lays the stones of the temple of man's life just, perfect and true.

4

Having been taught that you are spirit and that spirit has to become master over the flesh, having been taught that God is all love and is caring for you, His child, hold fast to this truth, and you will 'bring forth good fruit,' both in your earthly and your spiritual life; you will demonstrate through the flesh something of the glory of the Father-Mother-Son, God, the Holy Trinity. Divine law is unfailing. Do not be downcast because things do not happen instantly. You must never doubt, because as soon as you do so you give power to the negative forces. However much you are tempted, hold fast to truth, and if men in the outer world sneer at you remember how ignorant the world is of spiritual life and power. Keep your own counsel; but keep also your faith in the living God, the power and life in you. By holding fast to your faith in this inward light it will grow even stronger; it will guide you to take the harmonious way, the way that will heal body and mind. With patience, my children, you will bring forth the fruit of perfect life on earth.

5

We want you all to forget the world and your body, and to realise you are part of God. You are spirit and you have a life in a spirit world which is superior to the material world. Always reach into the spiritual life. Bring into your earthly life the gentleness, the beauty, of your true, your spiritual nature, which is part of the divine nature, part of God. The Master Jesus said, 'Be ye perfect, even as your Father in heaven is perfect'; meaning —know (in your innermost being) that you *are* perfect in God. He said, 'I and the Father are one.' He teaches all his brethren on earth to follow this path of truth; to understand that they and the Father are indeed one, that God is the Creator of all life. He would have you realise that God is in you, and that you have within yourself the power to create the perfect life on earth, through realisation of that perfect spirit in you, which is at one with the Father.

III

Creative Thought

Remember, brethren, what we have told you of the cause of disease and the source of all healing; remember also that your habitual thoughts either create or destroy. Lack of harmony in your thoughts or in your life brings disease; harmony brings health. Therefore let go all resentment, fear and criticism. Hold only the positive thought of all-good, God, and light will flow into you.

Do things so much matter? The disorder of the material life may rage all round you, but it cannot enter your temple, it cannot reach the holy place within you unless you allow it to do so.

One of the lessons which the candidate on the path to spiritual illumination has to learn is that nothing can really touch or hurt him. The natural physical instinct is to fear, but the spirit of truth within you has to bring through into full consciousness the knowledge that no harm can touch the real you. Encourage this thought until it is always with you. Nothing can harm you and there is nothing to fear except fear. If you have

wrong

there is nothing to fear — accept fear.

full confidence in God the white light will flow through your being and all darkness will be eliminated. Live quietly, tranquilly, in God's love. Every life which is of God is crowned by love, which is a supreme and perfect happiness.

2

When you concentrate upon negative things you give them life, but if you cease to think about them you withdraw life from them and they gradually die. People say: 'Oh, but we do not want to turn our backs on reality, we must face it.' But, my children, reality is light, reality is all that is positive, good, pure and true. It is what you call evil that is unreal. Always concentrate on goodness, beauty and love.

Do you remember the story of the Master and his disciples who were passing a dead animal? The disciples were shocked and exclaimed with horror at the appearance of the dead body, but the Master did not see anything repellent in the sight. He just said, 'How white are his teeth!'

There is always something beautiful to be found. Look for it: concentrate on it. This positive loving attitude towards life and people helps you to perceive the divine essence, to put into operation the divine magic which heals.

3

When thoughts of depression, fear and anxiety creep on you, you say these are only natural and human: but the truth is that you are picking up such thoughts because you attract them. Man is like a magnet, he draws to himself angels of creative light, or angels of darkness and destruction. The angels of light come close to those who humbly and truly seek to serve the Great White Spirit.

The purpose of man's life is that he shall grow towards consciousness of his own God-qualities, and the way to do this is for him continually to rise in thought to the spheres of light, continually to open himself to the constructive forces and creative power of God.

It is one thing to learn about scientific facts, or to study spiritual or occult truth; but until you have *built into your soul body* the light-atoms, the constructive God-atoms, you cannot serve life as you would like to serve. It is one thing to know with your mind and another to *know with your inner self*; and to know with your inner self implies spontaneous good thought and spontaneous good action, spontaneous giving forth of that light which is Love, which is creative, which is quickening the very vibrations of your world and your physical body.

We often say that all things will work out eventually for your comfort and peace and happiness; but you must work as well as pray, and you must also daily partake of an inner communion. You know this; but the demands of modern life seem so urgent that you forget the grave importance and need of this inner communion, the breaking of the bread of life. This, together with loving service in the world, will build into your being particles of light, transmute the darkness, and overcome destructive forces which play around and within you. This is the secret of the transmutation of the dark, dull, heavy metals of gross matter into the pure gold of spirit.

4

We would impress upon you again the importance of continual effort towards good thought, for such thought not only builds man's spiritual bodies but also refines his physical body.

Right thought is based on God; it is God-thought. What man thinks today he becomes tomorrow; he daily re-creates his body, his life, his soul, and builds his spiritual achievement, through thought. Right thought, God-thought, requires self-discipline, and the effort is too much

for most people; but do remember the importance of steadily 'keeping on keeping on'; for the
man who sees his goal and works steadfastly
towards it attains perfect health and happiness.

Your life should be lived in God-thought.
Look for good, believe in good, trust in good.
Never cease to think charitably of your neighbour
and of the world. You will be surprised at what
will result.

When you feel little aches and pains, instead
of encouraging them and nurturing them, put
in their place a perfect thought, a God-thought.
We know this is a gospel of perfection; but we
know, too, that until man puts this into daily
practice he will continue in muddle and confusion.

5

A life controlled by positive good thought, a
life directed from the heart or from the Christ
spirit, is well-ordered, peaceful, harmonious,
happy. Nothing disturbs it. Gentle, beautiful and
harmonious order makes all things new, all
things perfect. On the other hand, the life which
is ungoverned, uncontrolled, unhappy, inhar-
monious, chaotic, comes under the domination
of negative thoughts, destructive forces. Yet, as

Jesus said on the cross, 'Father, forgive them; for they know not what they do.' It is ignorance which brings chaos. Ignorance is itself chaotic, undisciplined darkness. When once the soul earnestly seeks knowledge and understanding, then it is set on a path which will lead to wisdom and harmony.

When all your thought is directed by the spirit, the Christ seed resting in the heart, when the thoughts are controlled and directed towards God, there must come a natural prompting towards right action. If the thought be right, the act must be right. Right action is God action.

Think good, eschew evil and all negative things: seek only for God, for good.

6

Again we say, cultivate tranquillity. This is not easy for some of you, because multitudes of thought-forms impinge on the sensitive aura and cause it to become like a restless and sometimes storm-tossed sea. Yet with effort tranquillity can and will be achieved. A Master, as the result of long training and the attainment of thought-control, can enter a crowded building or walk in a public thoroughfare and yet remain as within a cloak, untouched by all the thought-forces which attack his aura. But this control is not attained in a moment, nor in a few weeks or months: it comes with steady, persistent effort of will over a long period.

The first step is to attract constructive atoms into your aura by constantly and resolutely putting away from you all destructive, pessimistic, and above all, fearful thoughts. Patiently strive to become attuned to the will of All-Good and this will draw to your aura positive, constructive atoms which will build a strong protective shell about you. But your shell will not be opaque; it will be transparent, translucent; the light gathered within you will shine through your aura so that all people will feel its warmth, and the kindliness, power and comfort which flow from you.

Another method which will help you to disentangle yourself from the babble of the world is to reduce your rate of breathing. Breathe as deeply as you can without any feeling of discomfort. Slower and deeper breathing will quieten all those agitated vibrations and build a protective influence into your aura. Next time you are in a public place or feel battered by the thoughts and emotions of the multitude, take a hold on yourself and breathe a little more deeply and slowly. You will be surprised at the inward power which will come to you.

Some of you may find that to visualise and concentrate on a star of light will help to still the restless mind. Or you may visualise your Master as you conceive him to be, perfect in form and feature, gentle, compassionate and shining with the light of heaven. It is good to create this image of your beloved friend and teacher and to focus your mind on him, for this will help you to express in your daily life all the qualities of the perfected man.

7

Many people ask how they can silence the intrusion of the daily mind in their meditations. We think the best way is to ignore the intruder. Do not worry about it; just concentrate more than ever on the God within. That concentration will become so absorbing and so powerful that the little outer mind will wilt and be unable to penetrate the enormous power of prayer to God. Concentrate your whole being on God until the realisation of His love becomes such a necessity to you that you desire nothing else. When desire for God possesses you and fills you with power and light, everything else will fall away and you will become a living force of God's light.

So also in dealing with humanity: when you have little difficulties and differences, it is far better to ignore them and let them pass. If you concentrate instead on the power and strength of Christ within, these foolish difficulties will disappear. Too much time is wasted in fussing and worrying; and you make mountains out of molehills. When you feel inclined to retaliate because you think you have suffered an injustice, remember, 'Justice is Mine, I will repay, saith the Lord.' You can safely leave to God the outworking of His laws.

Remember also that your fellow travellers on life's road are confused, as you are, by the events which occur in human life; they are confused by emotions and desires which they do not understand. Every soul is striving, even as you are; so train yourself to look beneath the surface of things, and you will find something true, Christlike, buried, perhaps deeply, but it is there for you to find if you seek. If you remember this it will help you to remain tranquil, loving and kind.

At the same time do not depend on earthly things or on people for your peace and happiness. Look beyond karma and confusion to the Eternal Spirit.

By concentrating on God and awakening the true faculties of your higher self you are doing all good, you are putting forth every effort in the finest and truest way. When you are in tune with God and love, you need not bother about negative things; they right themselves.

IV

Divine Law, and Solvent of all Pain

Every soul must surrender soon or late to the divine law, which is love, and rules all, not only physical life but the spheres beyond, and all worlds in space. Nothing can escape it. It is God, the motive power which turns the wheels of human and cosmic life. If you have a problem you can solve it if you surrender your mind to Christ; not to the individual Christ but to the breathing, living, universal Christ Spirit. If you do this your problem will solve itself. When in difficulties, apply this law and you will unfailingly receive the answer to your problem.

You are all very dear to our hearts; we watch over you and we understand your problems, but we do not see them quite in the same light as you do; it is our work to tend your spirits, to raise you in consciousness to a world of light and peace which is outside the conflict and depression of physical life. Whatever your problems are, do remember that God holds the plan, and there is a just and perfect outworking of human karma. At the same time, take care that you do not make fresh difficult karma. You must be continually making karma, but remember that what you did yesterday is past. What you do today and every day is making the future. You are making conditions on earth and in heaven. You can be sowing the seeds of good karma whose harvest will be a new age of gold. You can daily walk away from the mists, and on towards the golden city.

This is no dream. In the past, now long forgotten and obliterated from the knowledge of modern man, there were golden cities where king-initiates ruled. You have it in your power to help with the rebuilding of those golden cities. *Live in the Light*, in the love and service of the Lord.

2

We would comfort those who are sad, those who are puzzled and perplexed. How can we best convey to you the love and wisdom of the Eternal Spirit? All things work together for good. A divine law pervades all life and good comes out of ignorance and darkness. There is a wise and merciful plan for the spiritual growth of men. If you are anxious about the future, dear brethren, we would reassure you that all will be well and that there is a wise purpose in frustration and suffering.

As we have told you, we know the sorrows of human existence because we have ourselves endured them. We know the heartaches, the disappointments of human life, its fears, doubts and terrors; we know also that behind the whole of human endeavour there is hope and light, kindled by persistent thoughts of kindliness and goodwill. We know that every grumble, every depressing, fearful thought can weave into your spirit-garment greyness and darkness, and ultimately darken your spirit, which should be a radiant thing. We know that on the other hand creative thinking will kindle it.

Every soul seems to suffer; but if you can see that suffering in its right perspective you will see that it brings a rebirth. Through limitation and suffering the soul emerges into the divine life and light, just as the insect emerges from the chrysalis stage into a beautiful winged creature in the sunlight.

Life is indeed governed by the law of karma; but it is a merciful law which ultimately brings to every soul indescribable happiness.

The wise man lets nothing disquiet him. He cares neither for praise nor blame. He does not grieve for the living or the dead. He knows that the divine law is just, perfect and true; that it will prevail in every detail of human life. Never grumble, never be discontented with your lot. If you will train yourselves to accept your karma, realising that you have much to gain from it, you will live so much more happily.

3

We know the sorrows and difficulties of life in a body which is at present unawakened to the beauty of God's worlds. We know how hard it is to walk in darkness, to accept the conditions in which you find yourselves, trusting in the love of the Great White Spirit, trusting that the eternal arms are ever around you and that your earthly experiences come for a wise purpose. This is not easy, we know; and because the brothers who have passed into the light understand the sorrows, the disappointments and the hardships of mortal life they come back with a great longing to help, to give you knowledge of your own inward powers, to tell you of those lighter and joyous states of life which await you. They want to tell you how worthwhile your efforts will prove; to say that no effort is ever wasted, although you do not see results. Keep on keeping on your path. We promise you that it leads to heaven, to a life so full of bliss and peace as to be quite beyond your imagination.

You will say, 'This is all very well. We believe what you tell us. But how is your promise going to affect our present-day difficulties and problems?' My dear children, we are pointing the way to your goal; and when your vision is fixed on it you will acquire a different mental and emotional attitude to your companions and the problems of everyday life. You and we know that the eternal Light is the great solvent; but to contact this Light the lower nature, which is of the earth, must be subdued, and mankind will not make the effort to rise in thought and aspiration to the life which is light and joy and tranquillity.

We come to offer you truth; to love you and to inspire you to look upward towards God. All your difficulties will then pass away; all are transient. No obstacle is insurmountable. Do your best. Do not worry about tomorrow. If your Father feeds the sparrows of the air and is aware of every hair on your head, He is aware also of your spirit's need and will not forsake you.

Earthly people live in a dense fog which only spiritual sunlight and the winds of heaven will disperse. A light burns within you which is turned down and grown very dim; you are the only person who can turn up that light and cause it to shine brightly so that the fogs of earth are dispersed. You can generate a power in yourselves which, like the winds of heaven, will sweep clean your surroundings so that all mists will disappear. The conditions of your life will change. More important than this, you yourselves will change so that the things of earth which have in the past seemed so tiresome will no longer have any effect. You will hold them in the right perspective, seeing they are unimportant. You are children of God, and God has planted within you power to be happy, to overcome all darkness, to enter into perfect life.

4

The ancient brethren used these words: 'Where hangs the key to the mysteries of heaven?—It hangs in the heart.' It is not merely a question of loving and worshipping God, and loving and serving man; infinite tenacity and strength are needed to hold fast to love, infinite love, God's love.

This love, placed in the heart of man by his Creator, is infinite power, supreme happiness; it is heavenly joy, unrealised at present. It is the power which controls the physical atoms. It is the power which draws to itself happiness and perfection of life. Man has to learn to use this creative power. If you would be healthy, which means holy, you must be happy. Search yourselves for that inner joy, that inner happiness which comes from knowing God.

The happy soul does not die of disease. Disease is the result of inharmony. Preserve harmony in your souls and it will be in your lives; your bodies will know no disease because every cell will be under the control and direction of God in you.

5

wrong

To love is to give without thought for self; to keep faithfully on a difficult path. Love is courage; trust; loyalty. Love is brotherhood expressed in every thought and word and deed; it is justice and right. Love is understanding of the other brother or sister no matter how deceptive appearances are.

Love is of the spirit and by it you recognise the spirit in your brother man. Love refrains from judgment, never attributes motives to another. God alone knows the heart of your brother man; you cannot judge. Love is kind, and suffers long.

Love is the solvent for every problem. Whatever it is, you will find that if you apply human and divine love to the situation your problem will disappear. With patience and love every human ill can be overcome.

The weakness is the self-will. The way is the same for all; those to whom you look for companionship and comfort have all passed the same way as you are now journeying; they have had to subdue self and let the light of the Son of God fill their lives. The gentle brothers are with you, and they neither judge nor condemn but pour forth pure love to strengthen and comfort you. It will light your way. As you receive this light from them and from God, do not cover it up but unveil it and give your love in the same selfless way to others and to life.

You all want to know what you can do to help those whom you know to be suffering either physically or mentally. You cannot prevent any soul's journeying its self-appointed path, but you can enfold the brother or sister with love, which is light. Enfold that soul tenderly in the light and talk to it on the inner planes; give courage through light, which is the spirit of Christ. This is love. Weakness or sentimentality is not love. Love is strong; love is true; love is wise; love is tolerant.

Love is the divine solvent of every pain and every problem.

6

The greatest gift you have is the gift of intuition; this is your true guiding light. But the intuition is so often overruled by desire. The voice of desire, however noble that desire may be, is not the voice of intuition, which works in your heart through love. The voice of intuition is subtle and is only heard in moments of selfless love, when the soul is attuned and at one with Christ.

//All the emotions of the personal life are in a sense tools which you use to fashion the temple of your soul. You learn through experience. You suffer through your mistakes. You buy your experience through incarnation; but if you know where you are going, and if you constantly pray for inner strength to keep your contact with the Supreme Sun, the spiritual Sun, the Christ Light, the Son of God, you will grow steadily in wisdom.//Through intuitions received in the silence and holiness of your own inner sanctuary you will get the guiding Light you need in your work.

V

Acceptance and Illumination

'Not my will but Thy will be done.' God's will for all His children is perfection on every plane; but man has to toil towards this perfection, and if it means returning to earth to correct mistakes, to work out the effects of a cause the soul has set in motion in a previous life, then gladly must he accept the law. If he is willing to endure that which by the will of God is the only way to correct past error, he must accept it joyfully; for acceptance in a spirit of meekness and love immediately wipes out cause and effect. The karma is finished. But acceptance must come from the spirit. It is not just a question of thinking about it, but of spontaneous expression in thought, word and deed. When the soul at last achieves this state of surrender it experiences illumination, an awareness of the golden glory of the Christ, a realisation that can never fade.

2

We are going to give you a very simple formula for health. It is this—*to live thankfully.* When a heart beats with thankfulness for its creation and for all life's experiences a light shines from the very centre of the being, which illumines the whole life. Life itself, the very zest of living and experiencing the simple gifts we enjoy through the five senses, should evoke an outpouring of thankfulness from the child of God; instead of which there is criticism, disagreement with life, and the heart remains shuttered. Yet deep within is the little flickering light, which when it is fed by the life-giving forces of the glorious sun, the Christ, will grow to a mighty fire.

Your burdens weary the flesh and the mind, but they will all be swept away when the heart opens in thankfulness for life's experience, for the sweetness and beauty it brings.

3

Beloved children, we in the spirit realms bring you all love. We cannot take sorrow from you because it is your experience, which will open your eyes to the beauty of the spiritual life. We cannot interfere with your karma, but we are permitted at times to give you a word which will help you on your journey: and when we see you taking a path which will bring you to heartache and pain, we are by your side, inspiring you with courage and strength. But however difficult the path, the way you have been led by the spirit, through your own heart, is God's way, and the right way. Knowing this, resign yourself to God's love.

When you are confused by life's problems seek your own inner sanctuary; humbly kneel before the presence of the Golden One. Do not let your earthly mind argue. Surrender yourself to divine law and you will have peace and joy; you will have no doubt that all is right, all is well. If you are in tune with God, you will know that God is love and God's way is always the right way. Trust Him and have faith. If you know you have been rebellious, ask humbly for forgiveness. This is man's only freewill choice—not whether he shall go this way or that way, but whether he will accept his experiences in love and humility, or whether he will be rebellious and angry, full of tortuous emotion.

4

Let peace fill your heart and mind and life. God never makes a mistake. If you do not understand, be patient and wait. In due time the light will shine and you will understand.

When we say 'Be at peace,' we do not mean a troubled peace. We mean a relinquishing of all earthly problems and resigning your life to God's

love. This is the way to the realisation of the
divine magic, the divine essence.

Some people think that to be peaceful and to
pour oil on troubled waters is a sign of weakness;
but let us translate the word as meekness not
weakness. The Lord Christ is meek; but he is
all-power, and peace is a dynamic power in the
individual and in the nation. The peaceful spirit
is powerful for good. Bring this peaceful spirit
through matter. Use matter; do not let matter
and your lower self drive out this peace, this
power, this divine love, this happiness.

When you have overcome and learnt to
dispose of the claims of the lower self and to
manifest divine love and gentleness; when you
have learnt not to retaliate or be resentful; then
the secret of the divine magic will come to you, the
magic which heals.

5

The Master enfolds you in his love, knowing your
heart and your need. But he knows also that the
problems and difficulties of your earthly life are
part of your karma, and he helps you by helping
you to command yourself.

It is not what is happening around you that
is important. It is the way you deal with such
happenings.

You can get worked up and make yourselves ill, as some of you have done, and may do again; or you can keep very still, and continually seek the place of silence and strength. Having stilled the emotions, the next step is to reach the innermost centre of communion and the in-taking of strength. You can then examine your problem and say, 'Dear God, I would have the strength to handle this as the Master would handle it.'

In the presence of the Master anger and resentment dissolve. You are raised above the pulls and antagonisms of the earthly plane. You are filled with peace, overcome with adoration and love.

If you are big and wise enough to do what we say, you will never again be torn by emotion, nor will you be puzzled; because there, within yourself, you will find the still, ever-burning flame, so bright, a flame of the spiritual Sun. As you concentrate on that pure, bright, white flame, you will feel the majesty of the Sun in yourself: you will know you are master of your body and the conditions of your life. Nothing can touch you. That Presence deep, deep within you is the I AM. 'Be still, and know that I AM God.'

When you can make that contact, my children, all your worries will fall into place; the pattern will become perfect.

6

We speak of acceptance; but on the other hand we say do not accept defeat or failure. Above all you must believe in the love of God, and know that with God all things are possible.

Some of you who have trained yourselves in meditation and in true worship have known the ecstasy of communion with the Eternal Spirit; and you know without any shadow of doubt of the goodness of God. Every soul learns in time that God is wholly good. There is certainly an aspect of the Creator which might be called evil, because it appears to bring suffering; but this is part of the process of spiritual evolution. We tell you without equivocation that the path of every living soul is upward, towards God.

You are being led on the right path by the ministering angels, messengers of God; all you have to do about your progress, health and well-being is to be steadfast on your path; you cannot alter your karma or anything else by being anxious, but you can alter a great deal by being confident in God. Hold fast to the certainty that God is love and that all is working towards a beautiful culmination. Concentrate on the life and light of God, and the walls of your prison house will melt. You can release yourself from bondage in the physical body by dwelling in spirit, in the Light; in the consciousness that you are in the Eternal Light and that no matter what happens God is with you. What happens to your body is not so important. It is what happens to you the soul, and you the spirit, that matters.

VI

The Higher Self

Beyond your physical body and the personality known to your companions on earth, is your true self which has descended from the spheres of light—your true home—to manifest on earth. It is impossible yet for that self to manifest fully through the lower vehicles, because they are not ready to receive that beautiful spirit; but you are preparing these vehicles, the emotional, mental, etheric and all the finer bodies, in your daily life. When through discipline and initiation your lower vehicles are ready, then your spirit will be able to manifest, to a great degree, through your physical form.

The higher self is composed of very fine ether and is pulsating with light, which as you develop will begin to shine through the chakras in the etheric body, the 'windows of your soul.'

When this divine fire is brought into full operation so that all the chakras are active as God intended, then the whole body will be in a state of ascension. We mean by this that the whole body, although still of a physical nature, will be functioning on a much higher plane of consciousness than it is at present. At present it may be in a dark state, but when the divine fire is kindled and active, then the body will be quickened in vibration and will be light and beautiful; it will approach the standard achieved by the God-men, the Sun-men, who walked this earth in the beginning of its creation.

Wise and great teachers are even now drawing closer to the spheres surrounding the earth, to bring their wisdom to mankind. Souls who have passed through the fires of suffering and who have attained a degree of self-discipline will be taught how *safely* to develop the divine fire within themselves; for it is both creative and destructive, and the ignorant and self-willed who think to use the mysteries of creation in a heedless and selfish way can bring destruction on themselves. Thus you will see the necessity for self-discipline and careful preparation of the finer vehicles; and also why those in the spheres of light who watch over mankind preserve the secrets until man himself is ready to use them, and to enter into the full joy of the God-life according to the will and purpose of the Creator.

Man in his ignorance is all the time dissipating this fire within him through his own urgent desires and passions, his uncontrolled emotion.

Every time you give way to passion and anger you dissipate this holy fire; every time emotions are controlled and transmuted to the warmth of love, you build the light into your vehicles. You are using the divine fire to illumine your own soul, to beautify the world about you and to glorify God.

Develop from the heart, meditate on love, live love, absorb love, give love, and your soul will become alight. The divine magic will rest in your hands enabling you to heal the sick, to comfort the bereaved, to bless the sorrowful, to beautify everything you touch, and to bring peace and happiness to the life of man.

2

The higher self of which we have spoken lies beyond earthly thought and beneath all sound and outward form. It is not approached through earthly thought but through realisation of the Christ Light. It does not intrude; it is not contaminated by the earth personality; it is wholly pure. When, in a flash, contact with it is made, cosmic consciousness comes, for when you touch the higher self you touch the whole cosmic realm. The way to approach this higher self is by surrender—surrender of personal desire, of self-love; and by contemplation, in a state of adoration, of the supreme being called Christ.

Every child of God must have within the heart an ideal of the Perfect One, but that ideal lies beyond thought. It is an ideal which embodies the purest realisation of what life might become, the purest manifestation of the son or daughter of God.

Let us put it another way. You create an ideal which is your conception of the Christ; you contemplate the qualities of that Being, you are aware of His perfect love, His humility, His purity; and as you contemplate you become identified with your creation. You cannot feel these qualities without becoming one with them, if only for a flash, and in *so doing you become at one with your higher self*, in fact with the Christ. We know you cannot retain that consciousness of pure light, pure truth indefinitely, for it is the very highest of which you are capable. But you can touch it in moments of exaltation and be illumined.

Your higher self does not usually function through your mind except when the inspiration comes for you to act in accordance with the laws of Christ; but the lower mind of earth is always ready to give you a good reason why you should not do so. In course of time you will learn to distinguish very clearly between these two parts of your being, the earth-self and the Christ-self. Again we would say that the higher self is not contacted through the mind, but through the heart and the quality of love.

Love is not possessive. To love is to give; love is a radiation, a sending forth from the heart of a sweet essence which heals.

3

All men can be servers, healers. All men can be consolers. What a lovely word! What more beautiful task can you be given than to console your brother, your sister? To be a servant of God is the most lovely opportunity given to man.

The practical servants are those who walk closely with God, who are ever aware of His Presence. This is the life which creates a saint; and all Masters are saints—humble, pure and clean. This is the state of consciousness for all who would heal, because as you aspire to it you create within you a power which men call miraculous.

Jesus in his simple ministry told the people to seek God. '*The Father and I are one.*' This is the source of healing power; when you are suffused with the holy light, the divine fire, through walking closely with God, the healing power pours from you. Never forget that of yourself you are nothing, and can do nothing. It is the power that works in you that accomplishes His will. This is important because God works as He wills, and not as you will.

In giving healing you must recognise that divine will which works through you when you surrender yourself to it. The basis, the core, the height of all life is God. Stimulate the God in matter. Seek the love of God, the will of God; never self-will. A hard lesson, when you are learning it! When you have learnt it, you will know that it brings the only enduring power.

'Thou shalt love the Lord Thy God with all thy heart, and with all thy soul, and with all thy mind.' There shall be nothing in life for you but God, the manifestation of God on every plane of your being, so that in all human relationships at whatever level in the outside world and in your own inner world you act by His will. This makes the perfect healer and the perfect man.

4

The star with the six points is the symbol of man made perfect, the Christed one. There are many Christed ones. They are those who have lived according to the Christ law. It takes many incarnations for the soul to attain to mastership of the physical, emotional and mental planes; but the man who can truly be called a Christed one is he who has trained himself to give love. In his daily life, in all his relationships with his brethren, he gives love; and love is light.

You all become confused about love and you say, 'There are some people I cannot love.' Our answer to this is, keep the personal feelings in abeyance. Love for love's own sake. Think how lovely God is, how lovely is His creation; and with all your heart and soul love God. Love the Christ.

Could you see healing hands at work with your inner sight you would see streams of light flowing from them. That light is the result of love. Only love heals—the vibration of love.

When you have an injury, think of the injured or diseased part with thoughts of love. Lay your right hand on the painful part and think of it in terms of love—love, not pity; pity is quite a different matter. Love the place, and the healing light will pour through your hand.

If we think of the suffering in the world with compassion, as we imagine Jesus thought of it, we can send forth a light like a great star which will find a resting-place in the heart of the weary, the sad and the sick; and there the great light of love creates a new life, a new body.

The projection of the light of the star to heal mankind should not be irksome or tiring; it should be a quiet radiation from within. You are the channel for the light. You yourself form the symbol of the six-pointed star. The I AM, the Christ within your heart, is the star, the flame. *I AM the star; the light of the eternal fires radiates through me and IS the star*. The star, as it radiates from your heart, calls to and stimulates the light and the love within the heart of those upon whom you are concentrating.

And now, using your imagination, imagine you are looking into the centre of that star which is the symbol of the Christ-man. As you gaze on it, concentrating on the love and healing light which it represents, you feel yourself being drawn into the star, you become part of it; and you are not only being healed yourself, but you are pouring out healing rays from its heart to the whole world.

The power of the spirit is within *you*. It is creative and knows no limitation. Never allow your earthly mind to cramp your thinking or restrict your vision. In your daily life, in your contacts with your fellow creatures, in your work, never allow yourself to feel the limitations of physical matter. You see, dear brethren, it is all a question of consciousness. As you think, so you *are*.

You are all accustomed to that phrase about 'building castles in the air,' without realising the truth of these words. Create in your consciousness, first of all, the star, realising that you are in the centre of the star. You *are* the star, and from *you* its light goes forth into the ethers. In doing this you receive strength; you receive the power of divine love, which does not admit failure. Divine love is omnipotent, omniscient, omnipresent. God is within your innermost being, and with God all things are possible.

At a Healing Service

Jesus said, 'I am the bread of life.' Now the bread of which He spoke is not of the earth, but of the spirit, given to the spirit within you by Christ the Lord. That bread is the divine spirit within you which through communion with the Christ is stimulated and becomes alive, becomes a power in you and in your life.

It is not mere fantasy when you are told that He is offering you the bread of life to eat. When you are truly prepared for communion, your mind is in abeyance, your heart is opening in sweet simplicity and love, and in that state you are able to receive the outpouring of golden light from the heart of the Lord Christ. This is the substance of the Cosmic Christ, the body of Christ, and this cosmic substance which you receive into yourself causes the divine life within you to grow and become stronger.

Therefore, when in spirit you partake of the bread, use your inner awareness, and realise as you eat that it is the Christ-life in you which is being fed. With your inner vision see Him proffer the wine in the chalice of gold—literally from the great heart of Christ. Try to partake of it consciously, believing it to be as real as any physical cup of wine.

For a time you are satisfied; but you should seek communion with Him often, for you need constant replenishment by that golden ray, to stimulate the Christ within you.

Beloved brethren, the power of God is with you. Set your hearts and minds on Him, and on heavenly realities. Put forth the divine will from within your heart to free your mind from all earthly sorrows, disappointments, pain, anxieties, from all earthly entanglements, so that you may rise in consciousness to be with Him in the temple of healing.

See with your inner eye what is prepared for you in the heaven world. See a shining company of angels waiting to receive the souls of those asking to be healed. See the sufferers being brought to the pool of healing waters. Go, yourself, with the patients who pass through the blue waters, and who emerge with smiling faces. See how you and they are now filled with the healing of the Christ Spirit.

Love, divine love, is the great healer. Love heals the bruised heart, the torn emotions. Love cools the heated brow; and you will see love personified in the form of the Lord Christ who comes into the heart of this healing temple. He comes in beauty and in gentleness, stretching forth His hand to bless, saying, 'I come that you may have eternal life.'

He offers you the bread of life. 'Take and eat; absorb the substance of my cosmic body.'

And now He holds forth the cup of wine to you, the wine of His spirit which flows from His heart.

'Take; drink; it is my strength, my life. Become part of my life. It is my love, and this love I give to you.'

'Drink, and feel the divine fire flowing through you, cleansing you from all confusion and pain. Be healed . . . and come up into the sun, into the eternal life of my Father in Heaven.'